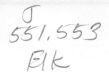

INVESTIGATING NATURAL DISASTERS

# INVESTIGATING
# TORNADOES

BY ELIZABETH ELKINS

**CAPSTONE PRESS**
a capstone imprint

Edge Books are published by Capstone Press,
1710 Roe Crest Drive, North Mankato, Minnesota 56003
www.mycapstone.com

**Library of Congress Cataloging-in-Publication Data**
Cataloging-in-Publication information is on file with the Library of Congress.
ISBN 978-1-5157-4037-7 (library binding)
ISBN 978-1-5157-4109-1 (paperback)
ISBN 978-1-5157-4126-8 (eBook PDF)

**Editorial Credits**
Alesha Sullivan, editor; Steve Mead, designer; Morgan Walters, media researcher;
Laura Manthe, production specialist

**Photo Credits**
Capstone Press, 6; Capstone Studio: Karon Dubke, 27; Dreamstime: Kathryn Sidenstricker, Cover;
Getty Images: AFP, 4, 5, Chris Clor, 13, New York Public Library, 19, Jim Reed, 25; iStockphoto:
sshepard, 15; Newscom: Shariful Islam Xinhua News Agency, 20; Shutterstock: Benjamin B,
29, Dean Kerr, 16, Dustie, Cover, Ernest R. Prim, 23, Justin Hobson, 11, Minerva Studio, 8, Nik
Merkulov, (grunge texture) design element throughout, cover

Printed and bound in China.
007883

# TABLE OF CONTENTS

# A PATH OF DEVASTATION

It was April 26, 1989. The country of Bangladesh was suffering from a major drought. The president asked the people to pray for rain. Just hours later the worst tornado in the world's history touched down in the Manikganj district. The tornado swept eastward, creating a path of destruction that was 10 miles (16 kilometers) long and 1 mile (1.6 km) wide. Bangladesh is one of the most heavily populated countries in the world. Most of its people are poor and live in weak shelters. The tornado destroyed every building within 2.5 square miles (6 square km). Twenty villages were destroyed, and 1,300 people died. Heavy rains and hail pummeled the district, and most of the people's crops were destroyed.

People in Bangladesh walk near ruins in April 1989 after a deadly tornado ripped through their city.

Tornadoes are one of the world's deadliest natural disasters. They often strike with very little warning. They can destroy everything in their paths, tossing buildings and cars into the air and flattening houses. For people in many parts of the world, the sound of a tornado warning siren is one of the most frightening sounds they'll ever hear.

# TORNADO BASICS

The sky turns dark in the distance. The clouds above echo with low rumbles of thunder. Thunderstorms bring rain, thunder, and lightning. Heavy downpours, strong winds, and hail are also possible. And a few thunderstorms bring something else—tornadoes. But how does a thunderstorm lead to the formation of a tornado? First, it's important to understand how thunderstorms develop.

## THUNDERSTORMS

**1**

Thunderstorms form when warm, moist air rises. An updraft of wind pushes the warm air high into the sky. The water vapor in the air cools and **condenses**, forming water droplets and a cloud. As more heat rises, a huge **cumulonimbus cloud** forms.

As water droplets in the cloud increase, the cloud can no longer hold in the moisture. The water falls as rain or hail. The air moving with the precipitation is called a downdraft. The downdraft is made of cool air. As the storm grows, more updrafts of wind and downdrafts may form.

**2**

DOWNDRAFT

UPDRAFT

**3**

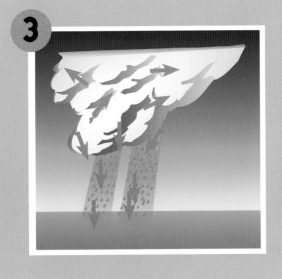

A thunderstorm usually dies within 30 minutes. By this time the rain and downdraft have usually cooled the air around the storm. Then there is no more warm air feeding the storm with moisture.

**condense**—to change from gas to liquid; water vapor condenses into liquid water

**cumulonimbus cloud**—a cloud that produces a thunderstorm

## Supercells

Not every thunderstorm generates tornadoes. Monstrous storms called supercells are the storms that most often cause tornadoes. These storms have strong winds that can create a swirling column of air. This rotating column of air is called a mesocyclone. The mesocyclone is typically 2 to 10 miles (3.2 to 16 km) wide. It can reach 50,000 feet (15,240 meters) into the sky. In approximately three out of 10 supercells, the mesocyclone forms a tornado.

The elevated winds in a supercell keep the storm going. The high-level wind blows faster than the wind below. This causes the supercell to lean forward. As the storm leans, the two types of winds are pulled apart. Because the downdraft winds and updraft winds are separated, the updraft winds do not cool down. Warm, moist air keeps feeding the storm, so the storm doesn't die out quickly. A supercell can last for hours.

a supercell

## Funnel Clouds

If a spinning mesocyclone starts reaching toward the ground, it is called a **funnel cloud**. And if the funnel cloud touches the ground, its name changes to a tornado. When a tornado moves across land, it picks up **debris** with its strong rotating winds. A tornado can travel miles across land. It may have a straight path or a curved path. A tornado's unpredictability makes it very dangerous. It can cause a huge amount of **destruction** in a short amount of time.

Scientists have several ideas about how tornadoes form. One idea is that the mesocyclone moves downward when the winds beneath it are weak. The slow-moving air below the mesocyclone is drawn upward and starts to spin. The spinning column then grows larger, pulling the air lower until it touches the ground.

A sinking current of air at the back of the storm may also play a role in the formation of a tornado. This downdraft of dry air moves toward the ground. As it moves, it may wrap around the spinning mesocyclone and pull it down. The rotating column of air stretches and gets thinner. Finally, the mesocyclone reaches the ground.

**funnel cloud**—a cone-shaped cloud that is usually a visible part of a tornado; a funnel cloud is wide at the top and narrow at the bottom

**debris**—the scattered pieces of something that has been destroyed or broken

**destruction**—what happens when something is badly destroyed

Tornadoes can form at any time of day. But they are most likely to occur in the afternoon or evening.

A tornado swept through Elie, Manitoba, in Canada in 2007.

# TORNADO ALLEYS

There are places in the world that are more likely to have tornadoes. The United States experiences the biggest, most deadly tornadoes. More than 75 percent of the world's tornadoes happen in the United States. They are especially likely to happen in "Tornado Alley." This is a name given to the area of the United States that includes the states of Texas, Iowa, Nebraska, Kansas, and Ohio. Tornadoes are common in this area because the land is flat. There are no mountains to stop warm, moist air from the Gulf of Mexico from moving north. It meets cooler, dry air coming from Canada. The meeting point of cool air and warm air makes thunderstorms more likely to develop.

## FACT

About 100 tornadoes are reported in Canada each year. Most occur in the south-central part of the country. Tornado season in Canada is from April to September.

Other places that see a large number of tornadoes are Russia, Canada, and Europe. The United Kingdom is sometimes called "the world's tornado alley." The U.K. is hit by more than 30 tornadoes each year. On one single day in the U.K. in 1981, 105 tornadoes were reported. However, most of them were not large enough to cause extensive damage. Tornadoes in the U.K. usually develop along long, narrow storms that form along cold fronts. Tornadoes along cold fronts are typically weaker than tornadoes formed from supercells, such as in the United States.

A painting shows the destruction of a twister tearing through London, England.

# SIZING UP A TORNADO

Weather experts have a system for classifying the strength of a tornado. Tornadoes are measured by their wind speed. Researchers can estimate a tornado's wind speed by the damage it causes. They consider damage to buildings, power lines, trees, and other structures.

Experts in the United States use this information to rank the tornado using the Enhanced Fujita (EF) Scale. The scale measures from 0 to 5. The more destructive the tornado, the higher the number. An EF1 tornado has wind gust estimates of 86 to 110 miles (140 to 180 km) per hour. An EF5 tornado has gusts of more than 200 miles (320 km) per hour. Most tornadoes are an EF1.

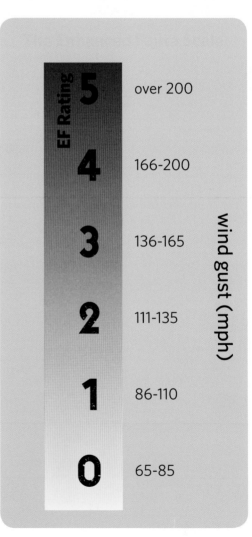

| EF Rating | wind gust (mph) |
|---|---|
| 5 | over 200 |
| 4 | 166-200 |
| 3 | 136-165 |
| 2 | 111-135 |
| 1 | 86-110 |
| 0 | 65-85 |

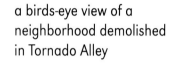

a birds-eye view of a neighborhood demolished in Tornado Alley

# TED FUJITA AND THE F SCALE

In 1971 Dr. Tetsuya Theodore "Ted" Fujita created the Fujita Scale. It was the first scale to measure the strength of a tornado. Fujita studied damage from tornadoes by flying over tornado-damaged areas. He inspected damage done to homes, cars, trees, and fields. Fujita used general terms to describe the damage, such as "well-constructed homes leveled." Later in 2007 the Enhanced Fujita Scale replaced the Fujita Scale. The new scale describes in detail the degree of damage done to structures. For example, if experts are studying damage to a large mall, they would consider whether the skylights and other fixtures were broken.

## Forecasting Tornadoes

Because tornadoes form so quickly and unpredictably, **forecasting** them as much as possible is very important. Local and national weather services monitor any approaching thunderstorms closely. They notify the public if conditions are present for tornadoes to form. A tornado watch means that tornadoes are likely to develop in a certain area. A tornado warning means that a tornado has been sighted. In places where tornadoes happen frequently, public tornado sirens often sound to warn people that they need to find shelter immediately.

Forecasters use tools such as the Doppler radar. The Doppler radar sends out radio waves that reflect off rain and hail and bounce back like an echo. Computers use this information to measure the storm's distance away and its intensity. **Satellites** can also take high-level photographs of clouds and storms. These images help forecasters locate areas with moist air where storms and supercells are likely to form.

## SEEK SHELTER

What are the warning signs that a tornado could occur or is approaching?
- dark, often greenish sky
- large hail
- a large, dark, low-lying cloud where rotation is likely
- loud roar, similar to a freight train

A Doppler radar can determine a storm's exact location using radio waves.

**forecast**—to predict or estimate a future event

**satellite**—a spacecraft that circles Earth; satellites gather and send information

# THE WORLD'S WORST TORNADOES

## In the United States

Because it sees so many tornadoes every year, the United States has also experienced some of the worst tornadoes in history. The worst U.S. tornado traveled through Missouri, Illinois, and Indiana in 1925. Nicknamed the "Tri-State Tornado," the deadly twister was rated an EF5. Almost 700 people died, and more than 2,000 were injured.

On May 20, 2013, an EF5 tornado touched down in the town of Moore, Oklahoma. The tornado was 1.3 miles (2.1 km) wide and stayed on the ground for 39 minutes. It traveled more than 14 miles (23 km). The tornado killed 24 people, including seven children in an elementary school. More than 200 people were injured. The twister crumbled roads and bridges and swept houses off their foundations. It was one of the costliest tornadoes in U.S. history.

**FACT**

The killer Tri-State Tornado in 1925 traveled 219 miles (352 km).

# COSTLIEST U.S. TORNADOES

| Date | Place | Actual Cost |
|---|---|---|
| May 20, 2013 | Moore, Oklahoma | $2 billion |
| May 22, 2011 | Joplin, Missouri | $2.8 billion |
| April 27, 2011 | Tuscaloosa, Alabama | $2.5 billion |
| May 11, 1970 | Lubbock, Texas | $250 million |
| June 8, 1966 | Topeka, Kansas | $250 million |

The Tri-State Tornado was the deadliest tornado in U.S. history.

# Around the Globe

The United States may see the most tornadoes in the world, but powerful, deadly tornadoes often happen in other countries as well. The loss of life may be greater in places without good early-warning systems to help people get to safety before a tornado hits.

People try to gather their belongings after a tornado struck the Brahmanbaria district of Bangladesh in March 2013.

# MAJOR TORNADO OUTBREAK

When several tornadoes form over a region, it is called an outbreak. The largest continuous and fourth-deadliest tornado outbreak in the United States was in 2011. A total of 362 tornadoes swept across 21 states from Texas to New York between April 25th and 28th. April 27th was the most active day with a record 218 tornadoes. The outbreak killed 324 people and injured more than 2,200.

In 1984 a severe tornado outbreak took place near Moscow in Russia. More than 10 tornadoes touched down in one day. These storms dropped pellets of hail that weighed an average of 2 pounds (0.9 kilograms) each. More than 400 people died. A couple tornadoes in the outbreak were powerful enough to **disintegrate** concrete that was reinforced with steel.

In 1989 Bangladesh experienced its worst tornado in history. The tornado was 1 mile (1.6 km) wide and injured more than 12,000 people. Around 80,000 people were left homeless. More deadly tornadoes hit Bangladesh in 1964, 1969, 1973, and 1977. These twisters killed a total of 2,341 people. The death tolls were high because many homes and shelters were fragile, and there wasn't an early warning system.

**disintegrate**—to break into small pieces

# STORM CHASERS AND SPOTTERS

Experts are always trying to find new ways to predict tornadoes and keep people safe. Some people specialize in watching storms and collecting information from them. Storm spotters are trained by the National Weather Service (NWS) to gather information about severe storms that take place near their homes. Then they report this information to the NWS. They report funnel clouds, tornadoes, the direction the storm is moving, and the estimated wind speed.

Storm chasers travel to severe storms. Some chasers are scientists gathering weather data. Some are photographers or news reporters gathering photos and information for a story. The chasers risk being hurt by debris or even killed when a tornado unexpectedly forms and they are in its path. Some storm chasers have special armored vehicles. The vehicles help them collect information but allow them to stay safe from being flipped over by the wind or hit by debris.

Tornado researchers study an approaching supercell in western Nebraska in June 2010.

# Climate Change

How will climate change affect tornadoes? Tornadoes are generated from thunderstorms, which feed on warm, moist air. These storms are created by low-level, unstable air. A warmer climate and warmer ocean water will create more of this unstable air. Increasing levels of **greenhouse gases** in the atmosphere also traps more heat on Earth's surface. This heat and moisture generate stronger storms and heavier rainfall.

Researchers have found that the number of days when large outbreaks of tornadoes occur has been increasing since 1950. And a larger number of tornadoes are occurring on those active days. With the world climate changing and shifting, tornado outbreaks could become more frequent.

**greenhouse gases**—gases in a planet's atmosphere that trap heat energy from the sun

A tornado can strike with almost no warning and destroy everything in its path.

# STAYING SAFE

Tornadoes can come out of nowhere. With some basic precautions and safety tips, you can keep yourself and your family safe. First, it is important to know where to go for safety if a tornado is headed your way. If a tornado siren goes off or a weather alert comes on the TV or radio, get to safety as quickly as possible.

If you are at home, you should go into the basement and get underneath something sturdy, such as a workbench. If there is no basement, find a small interior room such as a closet or bathroom. Stay away from windows. Crouch down, and cover your head with your hands.

If you live in a mobile home, do not stay there. Go to a tornado shelter or a sturdy building nearby. If you are caught outside, find a ditch or a low place and lie down on your stomach. Cover your head with your hands.

**FACT**

Injuries from flying debris cause the most tornado-related deaths.

It is important to protect your head and face from falling or flying debris during a tornado.

## Safety in the Aftermath

A tornado often leaves behind piles of broken wood and jagged pieces of metal. There can be sharp objects in the rubble and debris left behind. Be careful when moving through tornado **wreckage**. Wear closed-toe shoes, long pants, and a long-sleeved shirt to protect yourself from cuts. Don't walk close to severely damaged buildings. These buildings are unsafe and could collapse.

After a tornado there is also the risk of electric shocks and fires. Stay away from fallen power lines. If you smell gas or hear a hissing sound in a home or building, get out quickly. Call the fire department or gas company to let them know a gas line might have broken.

Nothing can stop a tornado from coming. However, being prepared for its arrival and knowing how to stay safe afterwards can help protect you and your family.

**wreckage**—the remains of something that has been badly damaged or destroyed

Do not approach fallen power lines because you could be electrocuted.

# GLOSSARY

**condense** (kuhn-DENS)—to change from gas to liquid; water vapor condenses into liquid water

**cumulonimbus cloud** (kyoo-myuh-loh-NIM-bus KLOWD)—a cloud that produces a thunderstorm

**debris** (duh-BREE)—the scattered pieces of something that has been destroyed or broken

**destruction** (di-STRUHK-shuhn)—what happens when something is badly destroyed

**disintegrate** (diss-IN-tuh-grate)—to break into small pieces

**evaporate** (i-VA-puh-rayt)—to change from a liquid to a gas

**forecaster** (FOR-kast-uhr)—someone who calculates or predicts weather conditions

**funnel cloud** (FUHN-uhl KLOWD)—a cone-shaped cloud that is usually a visible part of a tornado; a funnel cloud is wide at the top and narrow at the bottom

**greenhouse gases** (GREEN-houss GASS-uhs)—gases in a planet's atmosphere that trap heat energy from the sun

**satellite** (SAT-uh-lite)—a spacecraft that circles Earth; satellites gather and send information

**wreckage** (REK-ij)—the remains of something that has been badly damaged or destroyed

# READ MORE

**Cernak, Linda**. *The Science of a Tornado*. Disaster Science. Ann Arbor, Mich.: Cherry Lake Publishing, 2016.

**Garbe, Suzanne**. *Threatening Skies: History's Most Dangerous Weather*. Dangerous History. North Mankato, Minn.: Capstone Press, 2014.

**Tarshis, Lauren**. *I Survived The Joplin Tornado, 2011*. I Survived. New York: Scholastic, Inc., 2015.

# INTERNET SITES

FactHound offers a safe, fun way to find Internet sites related to this book. All of the sites on FactHound have been researched by our staff.

Here's all you do:

Visit *www.facthound.com*

Type in this code: 9781515740377

Check out projects, games and lots more at
**www.capstonekids.com**

# CRITICAL THINKING USING THE COMMON CORE

1. What specific conditions are needed for a tornado to form? (Key Ideas and Details)

2. How are tornadoes measured? Describe the system. (Key Ideas and Details)

3. How could climate change affect the weather? (Key Ideas and Details)

# INDEX